FRIENDS
OF ACPL

Gone Forever!

Apatosaurus

Rupert Matthews

Heinemann Library
Chicago, Illinois

Customer Service 888-454-2279
Visit our website at www.heinemannlibrary.com

Produced for Heinemann Library by White-Thomson Publishing Ltd.
Edited by Kay Barnham
Book design by John Jamieson
Concept design by Ron Kamen and Paul Davies & Associates
Illustrations by James Field (SGA)
Originated by Que-Net Media™
Printed and bound in China by South China Printing Company

08 07 06 05 04
10 9 8 7 6 5 4 3 2 1

Library of Congress Cataloging-in-Publication Data
Matthews, Rupert.
  Apatosaurus / Rupert Matthews.
    p. cm. -- (Gone forever!)
Summary: Discusses the apatosaurus dinosaur, including its known physical characteristics, behavior, habitat, and what other creatures were contemporaneous with it, as well as how scientists study fossils and evaluate geological features to learn about extinct organisms. Includes bibliographical references and index.
  ISBN 1-4034-4910-4 (hardcover) -- ISBN 1-4034-4917-1 (pbk.)
  1. Apatosaurus--Juvenile literature. [1. Apatosaurus. 2. Dinosaurs.]
I. Title.
  QE862.S3M3323 2004
  567.913'8--dc22

                           2003016682

Acknowledgments
The author and publisher are grateful to the following for permission to reproduce copyright material:
Cover photograph reproduced with permission of Corbis.
pp. 4, 10, 26 Natural History Museum, London; p. 6 Geoscience; p. 8 M. Nimmo/Frank Lane Picture Agency; pp. 12, 24 Corbis; pp. 14, 18 Sinclair Stammers/Science Photo Library; p. 16 Royal Tyrrell Museum/Alberta Community Development; p. 20 Carnegie Museum, Pittsburgh; p. 22 David Hosking/Frank Lane Picture Library.

Special thanks to Dr. Peter Makovicky of the Chicago Field Museum for his review of this book.

Every effort has been made to contact copyright holders of any material reproduced in this book. Any omissions will be rectified in subsequent printings if notice is given to the publisher.

Some words are shown in bold, **like this.** You can find out what they mean by looking in the glossary.

Contents

Gone Forever!

Many animals that lived long ago are **extinct.** This means that none of them are alive today. Scientists learn about extinct animals by studying their **fossils,** which are found in rocks.

Camptosaurus

Apatosaurus

Stegosaurus

Apatosaurus was a type of **dinosaur** that lived
millions of years ago. Other types of dinosaurs
were alive at the same time as Apatosaurus.
They are all now extinct.

5

Apatosaurus' Home

Apatosaurus **fossils** have been found in rocks in North America. Scientists called **geologists** stud these **ancient** rocks. They look for clues that sho them what the world was like when Apatosaurus was alive.

Apatosaurus lived in an area that was flat and wet. There were wide rivers and large lakes. **Ferns** and bushes grew all around, with trees dotted here and there. The weather was warm and wet.

Plants and Trees

Near the **fossils** of Apatosaurus, scientists also found plant fossils. These fossils show what plants grew at the time of Apatosaurus. Some of these plants are **extinct.** Other plants were like plants that grow today.

leaf fossil

Plant fossils show that Apatosaurus' world was a very green place. Many different kinds of **ferns** grew. There were **fir** and **pine** trees, too. None of the plants had flowers or fruits.

Living with Apatosaurus

While Apatosaurus lived, life on Earth went through some big changes. This was a time when many creatures first appeared, including a **mammal** called **Megazostrodon.**

Megazostrodon fossil

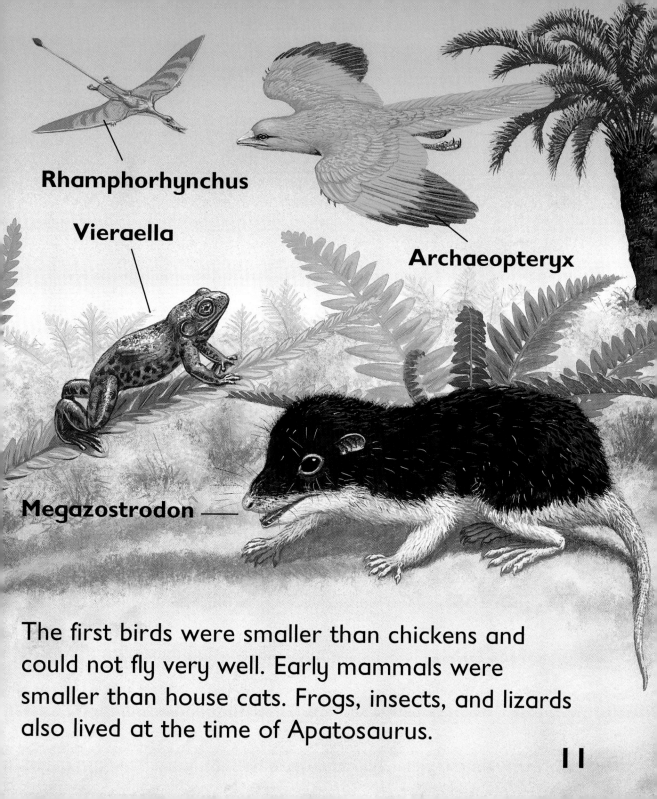

Rhamphorhynchus

Vieraella

Archaeopteryx

Megazostrodon ——

The first birds were smaller than chickens and could not fly very well. Early mammals were smaller than house cats. Frogs, insects, and lizards also lived at the time of Apatosaurus.

What Was Apatosaurus?

Scientists who study **fossils** are called **paleontologists.** Apatosaurus fossils have shown paleontologists that this **dinosaur** was one of the largest of them all. It was about three times as big as an elephant!

Apatosaurus was too large and heavy to move
very quickly. The shape of its teeth shows
scientists that this dinosaur ate plants.

Baby Apatosaurus

dinosaur egg fossils

Apatosaurus laid eggs instead of giving birth to live young. The mother **dinosaur** probably kept her eggs safe by burying them in an underground nest. This meant that they would be out of reach of dinosaurs that fed on eggs.

The Apatosaurus babies **hatched** several weeks after the eggs were laid. Then they would dig their way upward until they reached fresh air.

Growing Up

Paleontologists have discovered that young Apatosaurus lived in groups. **Dinosaurs** that **hatched** from the same nest may have stayed together, growing up with their brothers and sisters.

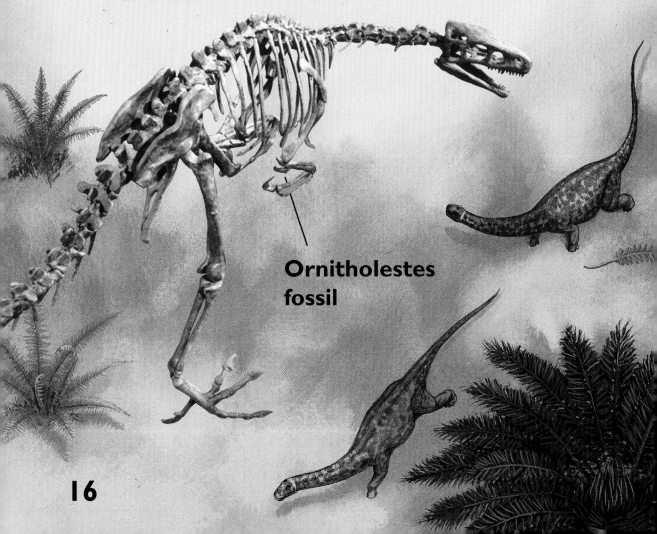

Ornitholestes fossil

It is likely that young Apatosaurus lived among bushes and tall **ferns,** where they would be safe. If they came out of hiding, they might be attacked by hungry **predators,** such as **Ornitholestes.**

What Did Apatosaurus Eat?

Dinosaurs as big as Apatosaurus had to eat a huge amount of plants every day to survive. **Paleontologists** have discovered that the most common plants of that time were **ferns** and early **palm** trees.

Apatosaurus had lots of short, rounded teeth. These were perfect for feeding on plants. The dinosaur may have bitten on a branch before pulling its head back to strip off the leaves.

Reaching for Food

Apatosaurus had a very long neck. Powerful **muscles** in its shoulders meant that the **dinosaur** could move its head around in all directions.

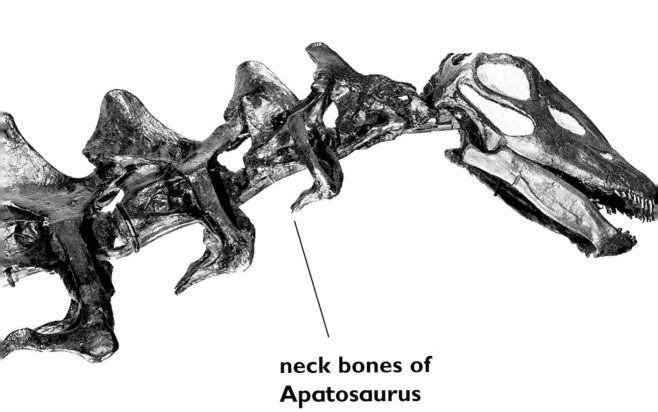

**neck bones of
Apatosaurus**

Apatosaurus' long, **flexible** neck may have allowed it to reach plants all around without having to walk much. This would have saved **valuable** energy.

Danger!

Paleontologists have found the **fossils** of other **dinosaurs** in the same rocks as those of Apatosaurus. One of these dinosaurs was **Allosaurus.** The fossils show that Allosaurus was a **predato** It hunted and ate othe dinosaurs.

Allosaurus fossil

Allosaurus grew to be longer than a school bus and was very strong. It used its powerful claws and sharp teeth to attack **prey.** Allosaurus may have hunted Apatosaurus.

Allosaurus

Apatosaurus

Fighting Back

A fight between **Allosaurus** and Apatosaurus would have been very **fierce.** Both dinosaurs had different ways of attacking. Allosaurus had sharp teeth and claws. It may have used these to bite and scratch Apatosaurus.

Apatosaurus skeleton

Allosaurus

Apatosaurus

However, Apatosaurus was much larger, heavier,
and stronger than Allosaurus. Apatosaurus
could have stamped on its enemy or fought with
its claws, scaring Allosaurus away.

25

Speaking to Each Other

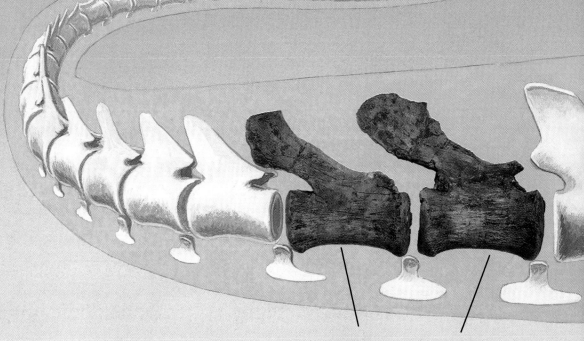

tailbone fossils

Apatosaurus had a long tail that narrowed to a point. Powerful **muscles** could swish the tail from side to side. If the tail moved fast enough, it would have made a cracking noise like a whip.

Apatosaurus may have used their tails to speak to each other. A crack of the tail could have warned other **dinosaurs** of danger nearby.

Where Did Apatosaurus Live?

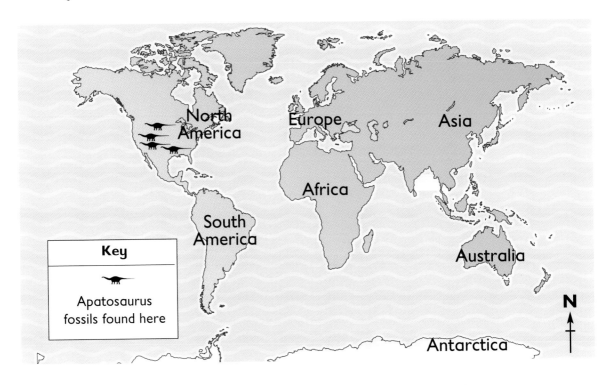

Key

Apatosaurus fossils found here

North America

Europe

Asia

Africa

South America

Australia

Antarctica

N

Fossils of Apatosaurus have been found in western parts of North America. When Apatosaurus lived, however, North America, Europe, Asia, Africa, and South America were actually joined together to form one gigantic piece of land.

When Did Apatosaurus Live?

Apatosaurus lived on Earth for several million years. It first appeared about 150 million years ago. It became **extinct** about 137 million years ago. This means it lived in the middle of the Age of the Dinosaurs, also known as the Mesozoic era.

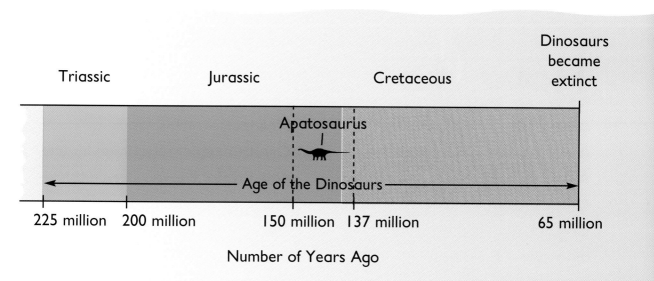

Fact File

Apatosaurus	
Length:	about 70 feet (21 meters)
Height:	about 20 feet (6 meters)
Weight:	over 33 tons (30 metric tons)
Time:	Late Jurassic period, about 150 to 137 million years ago
Place:	North America

How to Say It

Allosaurus—al-o-sawr-us

Apatosaurus—ah-pat-o-sawr-us

Archaeopteryx—ar-key-op-ter-iks

Camptosaurus—kamp-to-sawr-us

Cretaceous—kreh-tay-shus

dinosaur—dine-o-sawr

Jurassic—jer-as-ik

Megazostrodon—meg-ah-zos-tro-don

Mesozoic—meh-so-zo-ik

Ornitholestes—or-nith-ah-les-teez

paleontologist—pay-lee-on-tah-lo-jist

prey—pray

Rhamphorhynchus—ram-for-ink-us

Stegosaurus—steg-o-sawr-us

Triassic—try-as-ik

Vieraella—vee-eh-ray-lah

Glossary

Allosaurus   large, meat-eating dinosaur that hunted other dinosaurs

ancient   very old

Archaeopteryx   one of the first known birds, which lived 150 million years ago

Camptosaurus   plant-eating dinosaur

dinosaur   reptile that lived on Earth between 228 and 65 million years ago but has died out

extinct   once lived on Earth but has died out

fern   green plant with large, feathery leaves and no flowers

fierce   showing violent, wild energy

fir   tree with flat, needle-shaped leaves that stay green all year

flexible   able to bend

fossil   remains of a plant or animal, usually found in rocks

geologist   scientist who studies rocks

mammal   warm-blooded animal with a backbone and hair or fur. Mammals give birth to live young that feed on milk from the mother's body.

Megazostrodon   very early mammal

muscle   part of an animal's body that makes it move

Ornitholestes   small hunting dinosaur that had strong front claws

paleontologist   scientist who studies the fossils of animals or plants that have died out

palm   tree with long leaves that grow out of the top of the trunk

pine   tree with needle-shaped leaves

predator   animal that hunts and eats other animals

prey   animal that is hunted and eaten by another animal

Rhamphorhynchus   type of pterosaur, which is a flying reptile that has died out

Stegosaurus   large plant-eating dinosaur

valuable   of great use

Vieraella   early type of frog

31

More Books to Read

Cohen, Daniel. *Apatosaurus.* Mankato, Minn.: Capstone Press, 2000.

Dahl, Michael. *Long-Neck: The Adventure of Apatosaurus.* Minneapolis, Minn.: Picture Window Books, 2003.

Gaines, Richard. *Apatosaurus.* Edina, Minn.: ABDO Publishing Company, 2001.

Index